Arduino

Practical Programming for Beginners

Table of Contents

Introduction

If you have ever thought of doing hardware programming, then Arduino is the best language for you to learn. If you have some basic knowledge of how to program in the C programming language, then it will even be easier for you to program Arduino. Arduino is the board which comes with sensors. The board has a chip or the microprocessor which is the one responsible for processing. It is the one responsible for processing the codes you write for the board, normally referred to as the sketches. Arduino is made up of both the software and the hardware parts. The programming itself is done on the software part, which is the Arduino IDE. The installation of this is discussed in this book. The hardware part is the one which is programmed, meaning that it is where the instructions are executed. If you have ever thought of programming a robot, Arduino is the best for you. Once you have set up the Arduino environment, then everything will become easy for you. Enjoy reading!

Chapter 1- Getting Started with Arduino

What is Arduino?

Arduino is the name for little electronic circuit board which can be programmed. The Arduino platform is based on hardware and software which is easy to use. The Arduino boards are capable of reading inputs, lighting sensors, turning on LED, activating a motor, and even publishing something online. For you to direct the board on what to do, you have to send the instructions to a microcontroller which is found on the board. This is done by use of the Arduino Software (the IDE) and the Arduino programming language.

Currently, there are hundreds of Arduino boards which are available for use. Arduino UNO is the basic one, and the one which is widely used today.

Requirements

Assemble your Arduino board, preferably the UNO or Duemilanove boards, and make sure that you get the latest version. Ensure that you have a USB cable of any length. The cable should match the USB connector of your Arduino board.

Preparing the Arduino Board

After getting the Arduino board out from its protective box, you should see the following if you are using the Arduino UNO:

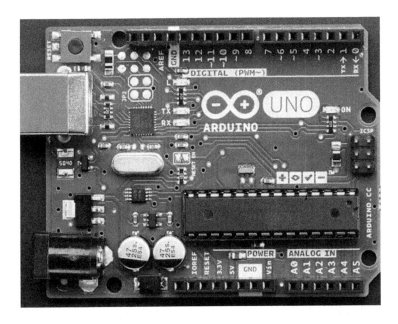

Make sure that it looks okay and everything is okay.

After that, if you have rubber bumpers, put them on the bottom of the board. These help you protect your Arduino board from any dirty tables and spills.

Parts of Arduino Board

We are using the Arduino Uno R3, as it is the latest version at the moment. Let us discuss its parts.

The Microcontroller/ Main Chip

This is the brain of the Arduino board. This is the part which is programmed. It is the one responsible for running the code, hence it can be seen as the CPU 9Central Processing Board) of the board.

This chip has some legs, which are usually plugged into the socket. These can be seen once it is taken out of the socket. However, they are not referred to as "legs" but "pins."

Don't worry if your Arduino board has a microcontroller with a different shape to the one given above, as this is common. Pins with a different shape from the one given above have pins which are smaller in size.

Power Jack and Supply

There are two ways that you can supply power to your Arduino board. You may choose to use a USB connector to establish a connection to a computer or a portable power jack, or you may choose to plug it into wall adapter. The USB can be used for powering and programming. The DC is only used for powering the board, and it is the best if you need to connect the board and leave it for a long-term project.

USB Jack and Interface

The USB Jack is the cable which helps you connect your board to the computer. You can use any computer, provided it has a USB port.
Some processor chips will fail when you are using a USB cable for connection to a computer. In such a case, you will have to use the serial interface. You must have a USB to the serial interface translator chip.

The LEDs

The Arduino comes with some lights from which you can draw ideas regarding what it is up to. The lights are referred to as LEDs. The Arduino board comes with 4 LEDs which are **L, RX, TX**, and **ON.** On the UNO board, you will find three of these at the center and one on the right side. The ON LED will turn to green once you have powered the Arduino board. In case you find it off or flickering, then just check on your power connection.

The RX and TX boards will blink whenever data is being sent from the board or being received on the board. The TX LED will light yellow once you send data from Arduino to the computer USB port. The RX LED will light yellow whenever data is sent to Arduino from the computer's USB port. The L LED is the one which you are able to control. The other 3 LEDS usually light automatically. The L LED has been connected to the main chip of the Arduino. This can be turned on and off once you begin to write the code.

Headers

This is the main part of the Arduino board. These are the two lines of sockets which line up with edges of the circuit board.
The thin sockets will allow you to plug in some wires into them. The wires can in turn be connected to any types of electronic parts including sensors, LEDs, displays, motors, etc.

USB Fuse

The little USB fuse protects the computer and the Arduino. There are high chances that all types of wires will be connected to the Arduino, which may cause an accidental short on the wires. The importance of this fuse comes during this time. It is resettable, and in such an occurrence, it will just open up in the same way a fuse or circuit breaker works. This will protect your board from damage.

Reset Button

This button is located next to the USB jack. However, in some other boards, you may find it on the right side. It is the button which can be used for restarting the Arduino board. Restarting the board will only take a second, and it is done if it gets stuck or if you need to re-run a program.

Power up Test

We are now ready to power on our Arduino board. You can simply do this by connecting one end of your USB cable to the Arduino board and the other one to your computer. The computer will act as the source of power for the Arduino board.If you are using Arduino UNO, then the USB cable should have its end as a square B-type.

The USB cable should be plugged directly to the computer port. After you are sure that you are able to power the Arduino board and then upload the sketches, you will be set. You can then plug it to the other ports. For you to know whether the power source is working correctly, just check on whether the ON LED is lit green. The L or yellow LED may also blink or light up, which the same case with the RX and TX LEDs.

Bootloader Reset Test

At this time, it is good for you to perform a bootloader test. You will then be sure of whether or not the Arduino board has been programmed with a bootloader. With the power source on, click the Reset button. The L LED should blink for 3 times so rapidly. You don't have to count the number of blinks.

Setting up the IDE

The IDE will provide you with an environment for writing your code when programming the Arduino. The software is open source. The Arduino software can be downloaded from **https://www.arduino.cc/en/Main/Software**.
This software is updated regularly, so ensure that you download its latest version.

Windows

In the case of Windows users, you should use the installer to install the IDE.

MAC

Download the application, and then drag it to a compressed folder.

Linux

The IDE software is available for both 32-bit and 64-bit Linux. After downloading the software, decompress it manually and then install it.

Installing Arduino in Windows

Ensure that you have downloaded the latest version of the Arduino from arduiono.cc. Once the installer is downloaded, double click it so as to start. Install it in the default location. It is highly recommended that you stick to the default installation steps. The installation takes less than two minutes to complete.

Depending on the Arduino that you are using, you may have to get and install some separate drivers for a USB to serial converter. You can download the driver installer and then run it.

Installing Arduino in Mac

Get the latest version of Arduino from Arduino.cc. Download the installer by clicking the link for Mac OS X Installer. Double click the installer so as to launch it.

Installing Arduino in Linux

First, visit Arduino.cc to get the latest version of the Arduino software. If you use the apt-get tool to install it, you will get an outdated version of the software. Click on the right version, whether 32-bit or 64 bit, and download it to the Downloads folder.

Open the terminal of your OS and then use the "cd" command to navigate to the Downloads directory. Use "tar xf arduino*.xz" so as to untar the package. Use the cd command again so as to change the directory to the new folder which has been created.

Install the software by running the /.install.sh command.

The "Hello World" Example

We need to make our Arduino do something by creating the "Hello World" example. In Arduino, this is just a blinking LED. From this section, you will learn how to load a sketch to Arduino board.

Begin by double clicking on the icon of the Arduino software so as to launch the software. The Arduino software should then be configured so as to make use of the right chip. You should first determine the chip that you are using from the Arduino board.

If the text on it says ATMEGA8-16P, then it is an **atmega8** chip. If the text on it is ATMEGA168-20P, then it will be an **atmega168** chip. In case the text says ATMEGA328P-20P, then it is an **atmega328p** chip.
Click on Tools, and then Microcontroller (MCU). Choose the kind of chip that you are using. Next, you should set the port. Click on Tools, then Serial Port, and choose the kind of port you are using.

Opening a Blink Sketch

Sketches are the small scripts which can be sent to the Arduino board so than an action can be performed. To open up one of them, click on **File menu -> Sketchbook -> Examples -> Digital -> Blink.** A new window with some code will be opened.

It is now time for you to compile or verify the code. This will get your sketch ready for transfer to the Arduino board. Compiling means that we are checking any mistakes and then changing it to an application which is compatible with the Arduino hardware. Click on "Sketch," then choose "Verify/Compile."

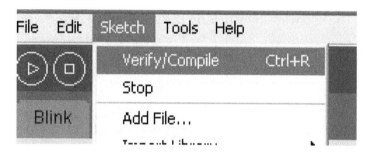

The message "Done Compiling" should be seen on the status bar after some seconds, as well as the Binary Sketch Size in Notification Area. This is an indication that our sketch has no error and that it can be loaded to the Arduino board.

The Arduino board should now be reset so as to prepare it for a new sketch upload. The new versions of Arduino don't have to be reset, but in case you are using an older version, then you have to do this manually. To do this, you only have to press the black button located on the right side of your board.

Uploading the Sketch

After all that, you will be ready to upload the sketch. Ensure that you have plugged in the Arduino board, you have selected the right serial port, and the green light is on.

Click on "File," and then choose "Upload to I/O Board." Wait for some seconds and you will see the message "Done Uploading" on the status bar.

Chapter 2- Sketches, Variables and Procedures

Now that you have everything setup and you know how to send your sketches to the board, you can begin to write your own sketches.

Blinkie

Begin by launching the Arduino software, and then open the previous example. The sketch should be in the area for text input in the Arduino software. The sketches are written in the C programming language. Here is the Blink example we had previously:

```
/*
 * Blink
 *
 *A basic Arduino example.  Turns on an LED on for
one second,

 * then off for one second, and this continues
 */

int ledPin = 13;          // LED connected to the digital
pin 13

void setup()              // run once, once the sketch is
started
{
  pinMode(ledPin, OUTPUT);     // sets digital pin as
the output
}

void loop()               // run over then over again
(looping)
{
  digitalWrite(ledPin, HIGH);  // sets LED on
  delay(1000);               // waits for second
  digitalWrite(ledPin, LOW);   // sets LED off
```

```
  delay(1000);              // waits for second
}
```

You see that there is some text written between /* and */. These are the comments. This is used to enclose multi-line comments. In the case of comments which take up only a single line, we use //. Comments helps one understand the meaning of code.

Variables

Consider the following line of code:

```
int ledPin = 13;          // LED connected to the digital
pin 13
```

This forms the first instruction code. This is a statement followed by a single-line comment. Statements end with a semicolon. The statement instructs the computer that we need to create a box, and then add the value 13 in it. The name of the box will be "ledPin," and it is of type int (integer). The declaration of variables takes this syntax, so we will be using this syntax throughout this book.

Procedures

Consider the following section of code:

```
void setup()             // run once, once the sketch is
started
{
  pinMode(ledPin, OUTPUT);       // sets digital pin as
the output
}
```

We have two comments, and each starts with a //, which denotes a single line comment. We have a statement at the middle which ends with a semicolon (;). However, the code is a good example of a procedure. A procedure is made up of many statements, as it is used to group a number of statements together so that they can be called by a single name. The procedure in this case has been given the name "setup" and it has no input values. It should also return void. Void is the programming way of saying nothing. This means that the procedure will not be returning anything.

The procedure has the following statement:

```
pinMode(ledPin, OUTPUT);      // sets digital pin as the output
```

Procedure Calls

Next, we have the following code:

```
void loop()               // run over then over again (looping)
{
  digitalWrite(ledPin, HIGH);  // sets LED on
  delay(1000);                 // waits for second
  digitalWrite(ledPin, LOW);   // sets LED off
  delay(1000);                 // waits for second
}
```

We have comments on the right side, and a procedure named "loop" which takes no input variables. It also has no output, as it has been declared using the void keyword. There are multiple statements within the procedure. The "delay(1000);" statement caused it to wait for three seconds.

To modify the procedure, change the input value for the delay to 500, of course from 1000 as shown below:

```
void loop()                // run over then over again
(looping)
{
  digitalWrite(ledPin, HIGH);  // sets LED on
  delay(1000);                 // waits for second
  digitalWrite(ledPin, LOW);   // sets LED off
  delay(500);                  // waits for second
}
```

After that, try to save the file, and you will get a warning that it is read-only. This means that you will have to save it using a different name. After saving it, compile it, and you will notice that the LED will be blinking at a much faster rate.

Chapter 3- Serial Library and Binary Data

It is possible for you to communicate from the Arduino board to the computer via a USB port. This can be done by use of a serial library.

A library refers to a collection of procedures, and all of these procedures are related. The serial library allows us to send data back to the computer, and we will be using it in this chapter. In serial data transfer, the transfer of data is done in terms of bits, one bit after the other.

For one to pass information between the computer and Arduino, they have to set the pin to high or low. The technique used for switching the LED on and off can be employed for the sending of data. One side will set the pin, while the one will read it.

Note that the size of data being transferred is measured in terms of bits and bytes. During the compilation/verification step, what you do is that sketch is converted into binary data. After you begin to upload the sketch to the board, it is transferred bit after a bit and then stored in the chip.

Create a new sketch, and then save it by the name "HelloWorld." Save the following code into the new sketch:

```
/*
 * Hello World!
 *
 * This is Hello World example for Arduino.
 * It demonstrates how data can be send to the
computer
 */

void setup()              // run once, once the sketch
starts
{
```

```
  Serial.begin(9600);        // Serial library set up at
9600 bps

  Serial.println("Hello world"); // prints hello
}

void loop()                  // run over and over, or loop
{
}
```

You can see the following line of code in the program:

**Serial.begin(9600);   // Serial library set up at
9600 bps**

The above is referred to as a library procedure call. The name of the library is Serial, and inside this, we have a procedure by the name "begin." This statement helps us to set the Arduino with the transfer rate which is needed. This rate has been set to 9600 bits per second.

The next line in the code is as follows:

Serial.println("Hello world"); // prints hello

This line is also calling the serial library, and a procedure named "println" which has been defined inside that library. This is the shorthand for the "print line." The text which will be printed has been enclosed inside double quotes.

You can now compile the sketch, and then upload it to Arduino. Click the icon for the serial monitor. This is shown below:

The common occurrence after clicking on that icon is that it will auto-reset your Arduino. You will see the sketch being launched after some seconds. In other switching to a serial monitor, you will have to click on a reset button, and then wait for about seven seconds for your sketch to startup. Click the reset button for more times and you will see this text appear more and more.

Suppose we need Arduino to print the Hello world text after every second. The following code can help us implement this:

```
/*
 * Hello world
 */
void setup()                // run once, after the sketch is
started
{
  Serial.begin(9600);       // set up the Serial library
to 9600 bps
}

void loop()                 // run over and over (loop)
{
  Serial.println("Hello world!"); // prints hello world
  delay(1000);
}
```

The code will print Hello world severally after each second. The delay(1000); statement helps us delay Arduino for one second before printing the text.

Now that you know how to print text, it is possible for you to print out numbers. Consider the following example:

```
/*
 * Math with Arduino
 */

int x = 5;
```

```
int y = 10;
int z = 20;

void setup()              // run once, once the sketch is
started
{
  Serial.begin(9600);          // set up a Serial library to
9600 bps
  Serial.println("Here is the math: ");

  Serial.print("x = ");
  Serial.println(x);
  Serial.print("y = ");
  Serial.println(y);
  Serial.print("z = ");
  Serial.println(z);

  Serial.print("x + y = ");      // add
  Serial.println(x + y);

  Serial.print("x * z = ");      // multiply
  Serial.println(x * z);

  Serial.print("z / y = ");      // divide
  Serial.println(z / y);

  Serial.print("y - z = ");      // subtract
  Serial.println(y - z);
}

void loop()              // this should be there though it
is empty
{
}
```

You can then upload the code to the Arduino board and observe the output. You will see that you can use numbers in Arduino, and even perform mathematical operations on them. Notice how we have used the "print" and "println" procedures so as to print on a single line. The latter has the new line character which moves the cursor to the next line while the former doesn't have that character.

The statement " Serial.println(x);" tells Arduino to access the value of variable "x" and then print it. Note that this has not been enclosed within double quotes. If you ask Arduino to do math, it can do it perfectly. The following statement adds the values of variables x and y:

Serial.println(x + y);

The input to Arduino is a calculation. It will have to backtrack and get the values of variables x and y, and then add them together. The result will then form the output.

A library "math.h" in Arduino provides you with a number of procedures which you can call and do some complex mathematical calculations such as square root, sin, tan, etc.

Suppose we have a right angled triangle. If you are given the two sides, you can calculate the hypotenuse. Below is the formula for this:

h = $\sqrt{(x^2 + y^2)}$

In Arduino, the value of h can be obtained by calling the sqrt function from the math.h library. Consider the following example demonstrating this:

```
#include "math.h"          // include Math Library

int x = 3;
int y = 4;
int h;
```

```
void setup()            // run once, once the sketch is
started
{
  Serial.begin(9600);        // set up the Serial library
to 9600 bps

  Serial.println("Calculating the value of
hypotenuse");

  Serial.print("x = ");
  Serial.println(x);

  Serial.print("y = ");
  Serial.println(y);

  h = sqrt( x*x + y*y );

  Serial.print("h = ");
  Serial.println(h);
}

void loop()            // this is needed even if it is empty
{
}
```

That is the code. The line:

```
#include "math.h"          // include Math Library
```

Helps us tell Arduino that we need to use math procedures found in the math.h library. The sqrt() procedure lives in this library.

```
h = sqrt( x*x + y*y );
```

The above line helps us get the sum of the squares of x and y, then find their square root, and this value will be assigned to the variable "h" for hypotenuse.

Chapter 4- Buttons, Switches, Digital Inputs, and Resistors

At this point, you should be able to make Arduino respond to the outside events. A push-button switch forms the most basic kind of input to Arduino. In this chapter, you are expected to have the following:

- An assembled Arduino board, most probably the Diecimila type.

- USB cable.

- 5 Red LEDs. A brighter one will be better.

- 6mm tact switch (the pushbutton)

- One 100 Ω Resistor (choose brown black brown gold). Any value between 20 and 220 ohms will be okay.

- Five 1KΩ Resistors (choose brown black red gold)

- One 10KΩ Resistors (choose brown black orange gold)

- Arduino Prototyping Shield having a tiny breadboard

- Hookup Wire

A switch can either be in the ON or OFF state. When it is in the OFF state, it means that you have disconnected the wires, while when it is in the ON state, the wires are connected. In this chapter, we will be using a 6mm, which is a 2-wire switch. These two wires are normally disconnected or open, but they are connected once you press the switch button.

Light Switch

We need to use the pushbutton so as to switch the LED light on and off.

Get out the Red LED and the 1.0KΩ resistor and tiny pushbutton, and then make a schematic onto the protocol.

Power up your Arduino board, and then press the button. Once you hold down the button, the LED should light. Once you release the button, it should go dark.

DigitalRead

Switches are good for control of current. However, they are the best when used as input devices. We will be setting the voltage on our pin to 5V or ground, and then using the DigitalRead so as to determine if our pin is HIGH or LOW.

We will begin by using a wire as the switch. Power your Arduino board, and then run the following sketch on it:

```
/*
 * A test program for a Switch
 */

int switchPin = 2;          // Switch connected to the
digital pin 2

void setup()                // run once, once the sketch is
started
{
  Serial.begin(9600);        // set up the Serial library
to 9600 bps

  pinMode(switchPin, INPUT);//sets digital pin as the
input to read switch
}

void loop()                 // for looping
{
  Serial.print("Read the switch input: ");

  Serial.println(digitalRead(switchPin));   // Read pin
then display the value

  delay(100);
}
```

You realize that Arduino has to be instructed to set the pin as its input. This is achieved by use of pinMode() but we combine it with INPUT rather than output.

pinMode(switchPin, INPUT);//sets digital pin as the input to read switch

We have also used the digitalRead() procedure which will help in getting the input from the pin.

Serial.println(digitalRead(switchPin));   // Read pin then display the value

The digitalRead() procedure will read and then return a result. The result can be either 0 for LOW or 1 for HIGH. This will be determined with what was seen after looking at the voltage of the pin. The pin and the value is passed as the input to the next procedure, which is println(). It is also possible for us to use a variable for storing the output from digitalRead(), and then this variable will be used as the input to the println(). This is shown below:

var = digitalRead(switchPin);   // read pin then save it into var

Serial.println(var);   // print out value stored in the var

At this point, you can use some wire to alternate between connecting the Pin 2 to the 5V and Ground through a 100Ω resistor. You can then watch the serial monitor.

You will see the serial monitor print out two messages which will be determined by whether the wire jumper has connected the output to HIGH (5v) or to LOW (Ground) voltage.

Iffy Statements

In the next step, we should be combining the inputs (the buttons) and the outputs (the LEDs). We will demonstrate this by making a light which is digitally controlled. We will write a sketch which is as follows:

If the button is pressed, the LED will turn on.

If the button is not pressed, the LED will be turned off.

Wire up the switch and the LED. Make the schematic shown below on your protocol:

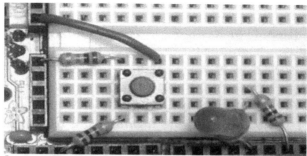

You can then write the sketch given below in Arduino and then upload it to your Arduino board:

```
/*
 * A test program for Switch and LED
 */

int ledPin = 12;        // LED has been connected to pin 12
int switchPin = 2;       // switch has been connected to pin 2

int val;              // variable to read the pin status

void setup() {
  pinMode(ledPin, OUTPUT);    // Set LED pin as the output

  pinMode(switchPin, INPUT);   // Set switch pin as the input
}


void loop(){

  val = digitalRead(switchPin);  // read the input value then store it in val

  if (val == LOW) {          // check if button has been pressed
```

```
   digitalWrite(ledPin, HIGH);   // turn the LED on
   }
   if (val == HIGH) {          // check if button has not
been pressed
      digitalWrite(ledPin, LOW);   // turn the LED off
   }
}
```

This is the first time for us to use the "if" statement. It is a logical statement. In this case, it helps us make decisions. The statement:

digitalWrite(ledPin, HIGH);   // turn the LED on

will only be executed if the "If" condition evaluates to a true. The conditions in this case are the "is the button pressed" and the "is the button not pressed." Note that for comparison purposes, we have used the (==), which should not be confused with the assignment operator (=).

It is now good that you are aware of how to turn on the LED once the button is pressed. However, if you have a TV, it would be tiresome to keep on pressing it so as to stay on. We need an alternating action switch, in which the press-and-release of the button will do something. We need to avoid the action of having to press and then hold the button.

For us to achieve this, we must keep track of the input value of the button so that we can know once it is changed. This is usually referred to as the "state" of the button. The action will be performed once the state is changed:
The following code demonstrates this:
```
/*
 * Alternating the switch
 */

int switchPin = 2;          // switch has been connected
to the pin 2
```

```
int val;                // variable to read the pin status
int buttonState;            // variable to hold last button
state

void setup() {
  pinMode(switchPin, INPUT);   // Set switch pin as
the input

  Serial.begin(9600);        // Set up serial
communication to 9600bps

  buttonState = digitalRead(switchPin);  // read initial
state
}

void loop(){
  val = digitalRead(switchPin);    // read the input
value then store it in val

  if (val != buttonState) {      // the button state has
been changed
    if (val == LOW) {            // check if button is
pressed
      Serial.println("Button has been pressed");
    } else {               // the button is not pressed...
      Serial.println("Button has been released");
    }
  }

  buttonState = val;          // save new state in the
variable
}
```

You can then upload the above sketch to your Arduino board and then watch the Serial monitor as you keep on pressing and releasing the button. The statement:

int buttonState;

Helps us create a variable which will be used to hold the state of the button. In the line:

buttonState = digitalRead(switchPin);

we are setting the value of the variable to the value read once we have started and the pin is setup to the input. In the code:

void loop(){

  val = digitalRead(switchPin);

we are reading the value of the state of the button and then storing it in the variable named "val." In the following block:

  if (val != buttonState) {

  if (val == LOW) {

We have two "if" statements in a nested format. This means that the first test should be performed, and if it evaluates to a true, we move to perform the second test.

In our first "if" statement, we are checking whether the current state of the button (LOW or HIGH) is different from what we had looked at in the last time. If it is found to be different (obtained by use of the != operator), we will execute the group of statements enclosed with the braces {}.

Next, we have an exotic "if" which is shown below:

```
if (val == LOW) {
  Serial.println("Button has been pressed");
} else {
  Serial.println("Button has been released");
}
```

Before running the test and if the test is passed, the statements within the braces {} would be performed first. We have an alternative which will be performed if the test is failed.

Counting the Presses

It is a good idea for you to add a way which will help you count the number of times the button is pressed. Write the following sketch into your Arduino software:

```
/*
 * Counting the presses
 */


int switchPin = 2;          // switch has been connected to pin 2

int val;              // variable to read the pin status
int buttonState;            // variable for holding the button state

int buttonPresses = 0;      // the number of times the button is pressed

void setup() {
  pinMode(switchPin, INPUT);   // Setting switch pin as the input

  Serial.begin(9600);        // Setting up serial communication to 9600bps

  buttonState = digitalRead(switchPin);  // reading the initial state

}

void loop(){
  val = digitalRead(switchPin);// reading the input value, store it in val
```

```
  if (val != buttonState) {        // the state of the button
has changed!

    if (val == LOW) {              // check if button is
pressed
      buttonPresses++;             // increment
buttonPresses variable
    Serial.print("Button is pressed ");
    Serial.print(buttonPresses);
    Serial.println(" times");
   }
 }
  buttonState = val;               // save new state in the
variable
 }
```

In the above sketch, we have added only one thing, which is the increment (++) operator. This will add 1 to the button variable (buttonPresses) each time the button is pressed.

Chapter 5- Keyless Door Lock System in Arduino

We will be making a keyless door lock system that will be using a 4*4 keypad so as to enter the keys plus a DC lock for opening or closing the door. The display will be done on a 16*2 LCD screen.

Requirements

Assemble the following components for the project:

- Arduino

- LCD

- 9V battery

- DC Lock

- 10k potentiometer

- 4X4 keypad

- 220-ohm resistor

- Relay

Once the keys have been pressed, they will be matched with the stored ones. The keys stored in EEPROM are "1234," so if these are matched, then the lock will open up. In case the match fails, then the message "access denied" will be printed on the screen.

If the # key is pressed, you will be allowed to change the password. First, you will be asked to type in the old password, if correct, the new password and it will be changed.

Making the Connections

Begin by connecting the 4x4 keyboard to Arduino. Connect the first 6 pins on 4X4 keypad to A0 and the A5 pins on Arduino. Connect the last two pins on the 4X4 keypad module to the digital pins 3 and 2 on Arduino. You can then connect the LCD to Arduino. The connections in this case should be done as follows:

- Connect pin 1 on LCD, the VSS pin, to the GND on Arduino.

- Connect pin 2, the VDD pin, to 5V pin on Arduino.

- Connect pin 3, the V0, to the middle of a 10k potentiometer and then connect your other two pins on the potentiometer to the 5V and the GND on Arduino. This is the pin for setting the LCD's contrast.

- Connect pin 4, the RS pin, to the pin 7 on Arduino.

- Connect pin 5, the R/W pin, to the GND pin on Arduino.

- Connect pin 6, the Enable pin, to the pin 6 on Arduino

- Connect pins numbers 11, 12, 13, 14, the data pins, to pins 5, 4, 3, 2 on Arduino.
- Connect pin 15, the LCD's backlight pin, to the 5V on Arduino through a 220-ohm resistor.

- Connect pin 16 on Arduino, the negative pin of the backlight, to the GND on Arduino.

Last, connect the DC lock to the Arduino. This lock operates on voltage ranging from 7 to 12V, meaning that we can't connect it directly to Arduino. To do this, a relay and battery will be required.

Connect signal pin of relay to the pin 10 on Arduino and lock's VCC and the GND to the 5V and GND on Arduino. On other end of relay, connect negative of battery to common on relay, then the NO on relay to one side of the lock. Connect the other side of lock to positive terminal on battery.

Keypad Lock Code

We will be using "1234" as the initial password. The code for locking the keypad is as follows:

```
#include<LiquidCrystal.h>
#include <Keypad.h>

#include<EEPROM.h>

LiquidCrystal liquid_crystal_display(9,8,7,6,5,4,);

char password[4];

char initial_password[4],new_password[4];

int i=0;

int relay_pin = 10;

char key_pressed=0;

const byte rows = 4;

const byte columns = 4;

char hexaKeys[rows][columns] = {

{'1','2','3','A'},

{'4','5','6','B'},

{'7','8','9','C'},
```

```
{'*','0','#','D'}
};

byte row_pins[rows] = {A0,A1,A2,A3};

byte column_pins[columns] = {A4,A5,3,2};

Keypad keypad_key = Keypad(
makeKeymap(hexaKeys), row_pins, column_pins,
rows, columns);

void setup()
{

  pinMode(relay_pin, OUTPUT);

  liquid_crystal_display.begin(16,2);

  liquid_crystal_display.print("Keyless Door");

  liquid_crystal_display.setCursor(0,1);

  liquid_crystal_display.print("Electronic Lock ");

  delay(2000);

  liquid_crystal_display.clear();

  liquid_crystal_display.print("Enter your
Password");

  liquid_crystal_display.setCursor(0,1);

  initialpassword();

}
```

```
void loop()
{
  digitalWrite(relay_pin, HIGH);
  key_pressed = keypad_key.getKey();
  if(key_pressed=='#')
    change();
  if (key_pressed)
  {
    password[i++]=key_pressed;
    liquid_crystal_display.print(key_pressed);
  }
if(i==4)
{
  delay(200);
  for(int j=0;j<4;j++)
    initial_password[j]=EEPROM.read(j);
  if(!(strncmp(password, initial_password,4)))
  {
    liquid_crystal_display.clear();
```

```
liquid_crystal_display.print("Password
Accepted");

digitalWrite(relay_pin, LOW);

delay(2000);

liquid_crystal_display.setCursor(0,1);

liquid_crystal_display.print("Pres # to change the
password");

delay(2000);

liquid_crystal_display.clear();

liquid_crystal_display.print("Enter Password:");

liquid_crystal_display.setCursor(0,1);

i=0;

}

else

{

digitalWrite(relay_pin, HIGH);
liquid_crystal_display.clear();
liquid_crystal_display.print("Wrong Password");
liquid_crystal_display.setCursor(0,1);
liquid_crystal_display.print("Press # to Change
password");
delay(2000);
liquid_crystal_display.clear();
liquid_crystal_display.print("Enter Password");
liquid_crystal_display.setCursor(0,1);
i=0;
```

```cpp
      }
    }
  }
void change()
{
  int j=0;
  liquid_crystal_display.clear();
  liquid_crystal_display.print("Enter Current
Password");
  liquid_crystal_display.setCursor(0,1);
  while(j<4)
  {
    char key=keypad_key.getKey();
    if(key)
    {
      new_password[j++]=key;
      liquid_crystal_display.print(key);
    }
    key=0;
  }
  delay(500);
if((strncmp(new_password, initial_password, 4)))
  {
    liquid_crystal_display.clear();
    liquid_crystal_display.print("Wrong Password");
    liquid_crystal_display.setCursor(0,1);
    liquid_crystal_display.print("Try Again");
    delay(1000);
  }
  else
  {
    j=0;
    liquid_crystal_display.clear();
    liquid_crystal_display.print("Enter New
Password:");
    liquid_crystal_display.setCursor(0,1);
    while(j<4)
    {
      char key=keypad_key.getKey();
```

```
  if(key)
  {
    initial_password[j]=key;
    liquid_crystal_display.print(key);
    EEPROM.write(j,key);
    j++;
  }
}
  liquid_crystal_display.print("Password Changed
Successfully");

  delay(1000);
}
liquid_crystal_display.clear();
liquid_crystal_display.print("Enter Password");
liquid_crystal_display.setCursor(0,1);
key_pressed=0;
}

void initialpassword(){
  for(int j=0;j<4;j++)
   EEPROM.write(j, j+49);
  for(int j=0;j<4;j++)
   initial_password[j]=EEPROM.read(j);
}
```

We have begun by including the libraries for the LCD, 4 x 4 keypad, and a library which will be used to store the password. The EEPROM library will be used for the purpose of storing the password.

We have defined the variable "key pressed" which will store the key which is pressed, which will in turn be compared with the other keys. If the # key is pressed, the function for changing the password will be called. The keys being typed will be stored in the "password" variable and will be shown on the LCD screen as they are typed. These keys will then be compared with the initial password which has been stored in EEPROM. If the match is successful, the lock will be opened and you will see the message "Password accepted" being printed. If the match fails, then you will be prompted to enter the password again.

Once you press the # key, the "change ()" function will be called. You will be asked to enter the current password for the system, and if found to be correct, you will be prompted to create a new password for the system.

Chapter 6- Access Control with RFID and Arduino

In our previous example, we used a keyboard for typing the password. In this case, we will be using a Radio Frequency Identifier Device (RFID). We will also be using a LCD display having 20 characters and 4 lines for showing the messages from the system. A servo-monitor will also be used for driving the mechanical device. The users will have tags or cards which are already registered, and these will allow them to access the system. The RFID sensor will access the serial number of the card, and this will be compared with the serial number recorded in the memory card or software.

If the serial number is registered, then the entry will be allowed. A green LED will light, and messages will be printed on the LCD screen. The buzzer will make a sound for access granted, while the servo will be moved so that it can release the mechanical device. Otherwise, the system will not release the access, the LED will light a warning red color, and a message displayed on the LCD display. The user will be advised to see the account manager. Let us discuss how the connections will be done:

Connections from RFID to Arduino Pins

- Reset > Pin 8

- SDA > Pin 10

- MOSI > Pin 11

- MISO > Pin 12

- SCK > Pin 13

- Ground > Ground

- 3.3v > 3.3v

Connections from Display to Arduino PinsVss > Ground

- Vdd > +5v

- V0 > one pin of the potntiometer | 2nd pin of the pot to the 5v |3rd pin to the ground

- Rs > Pin 7

- R/w > Ground

- E > Pin 6

- D0,D1,D2,D3 > no connection

- D4 > Pin 5

- D5 > Pin 4

- D6 > Pin 3

- D7 > Pin 2

- A > +5v

- K > ground

Connections from SERVO to Arduino Pins

- Control pin > Pin 9

- Vcc > +5v

- Ground > Ground

Connections from BUZZER to Arduino Pins

- Positive pin > Pin A2

- Ground > Ground

Connections from GREEN LED to Arduino Pins

- Positive pin > Pin A1

- Ground > Ground

The connections should be done as per the directions given above, so ensure that you do so. After that, load the following sketch to your Arduino board:

```
#include <LiquidCrystal.h> // the LCD library
#include <Servo.h> // the servo library
int servoPin = 9;
Servo Servo1;

LiquidCrystal lcd(7, 6, 5, 4, 3, 2);

int red=A0;
int green=A1;

#include <MFRC522.h> // The RFID Library
#include <SPI.h> // For communication via the SPI
with Module

#define SDAPIN 10 // the RFID Module SDA Pin has
been connected to UNO 10 Pin

#define RESETPIN 8 // the RFID Module RST Pin has
been connected to UNO 8 Pin

byte FoundTag; // Variable for checking if the Tag was
found
byte ReadTag; // Variable for storing anti-collision
value for reading Tag information
```

```
byte TagData[MAX_LEN]; // Variable for storing Full
Tag Data

byte TagSerialNumber[5]; // Variable for storing only
Tag Serial Number

byte GoodTagSerialNumber[5] = {0x0E, 0x4A, 0x79,
0x21};
// The Tag S/N. will give the rfid tag identity code here

MFRC522 nfc(SDAPIN, RESETPIN);
// Init of library using UNO pins declared above

void setup() {
Servo1.attach(servoPin);
pinMode(A0, OUTPUT);
pinMode(A1, OUTPUT);
pinMode(A2, OUTPUT);
lcd.begin(20, 4);
  // Print message to the LCD.
lcd.setCursor(0,0);
lcd.print("RFID SECURITY SYSTEM");
delay(200);
lcd.setCursor(2,1);
lcd.print(" PROJECT DONE BY  ");
delay(200);
lcd.setCursor(0,3);
lcd.print(" S6 ELS 2014-2017");
delay(1000);
lcd.setCursor(0,2);
lcd.print("   LIJIN ASHOK  ");
delay(2000);
lcd.setCursor(0,2);
lcd.print("    MIDHUN M S");
delay(2000);
lcd.setCursor(0,2);
lcd.print("    PRABHU Y RAJ");
delay(2000);
lcd.setCursor(0,2);
```

```
lcd.print("    SARATH P ");
delay(2000);
lcd.setCursor(0,2);
lcd.print("    SREEJITH R S ");
delay(2000);
pinMode(red, OUTPUT);
pinMode(green, OUTPUT);
SPI.begin();
Serial.begin(9600);

// Start to find the RFID Module
Serial.println("Looking for the RFID Reader");
nfc.begin();

byte version = nfc.getFirmwareVersion(); // Variable
for storing Firmware version of Module

// If it can't find the RFID Module
if (! version) {
Serial.print("Didn't find the RC522 board.");
while(1); //Wait until RFID Module has been found
}

// If found, print the information about the RFID
Module
Serial.print("Found chip RC522 ");
Serial.print("Firmware version: 0x");
Serial.println(version, HEX);
Serial.println();
}

void loop() {
 Servo1.write(0);
 delay(300);
lcd.clear();
lcd.setCursor(0,0);
lcd.print("RFID SECURITY SYSTEM");
lcd.setCursor(4,3);
lcd.print("SHOW YOUR ID");
```

```
lcd.noDisplay();
delay(200);
lcd.display();
delay(250);

String GoodTag="False"; // Variable used for
confirming good Tag Detected

// Check whether the Tag was detected
// If yes, the variable FoundTag will have "MI_OK"
FoundTag = nfc.requestTag(MF1_REQIDL, TagData);

if (FoundTag == MI_OK) {
delay(200);

//Get the anti-collision value to read information
from Tag
ReadTag = nfc.antiCollision(TagData);

memcpy(TagSerialNumber, TagData, 4); // Write Tag
information in TagSerialNumber variable

Serial.println("Tag detected.");
Serial.print("Serial Number: ");

for (int i = 0; i < 4; i++) { // Loop to print the serial
number to the serial monitor

Serial.print(TagSerialNumber[i], HEX);
Serial.print(", ");
}
Serial.println("");
Serial.println();


// Check if the detected Tag has right Serial number
for(int i=0; i < 4; i++){
```

```
if (GoodTagSerialNumber[i] != TagSerialNumber[i])
{
break;
}
if (i == 3) {
GoodTag="TRUE";
}
}
if (GoodTag == "TRUE"){
 lcd.clear();
 lcd.setCursor(0,0);
lcd.print("RFID SECURITY SYSTEM");
 lcd.setCursor(3, 1);
 lcd.print("ACCESS GRANTED");
 lcd.setCursor(0,3);
 digitalWrite(A1, HIGH);
 lcd.print(" +----WELCOME----+");
 digitalWrite(A2, HIGH);
 delay(300);
digitalWrite(A2, LOW);
 delay(300);
 digitalWrite(A2, HIGH);
 delay(300);
 digitalWrite(A2, LOW);
 delay(300);
 digitalWrite(A2, HIGH);
 delay(300);
 digitalWrite(A2, LOW);
 delay(300);
 digitalWrite(A2, HIGH);
 delay(300);
 digitalWrite(A2, LOW);
 delay(300);
 digitalWrite(A2, HIGH);
 delay(300);
 digitalWrite(A2,LOW);
 Servo1.write(180);
delay(7000);
Servo1.write(0);
```

```
  digitalWrite(A1, LOW);
}
else {
 lcd.clear();
 lcd.setCursor(0,0);
lcd.print("RFID SECURITY SYSTEM");
 lcd.setCursor(3, 1);
 lcd.print("ACCESS DENIED");
digitalWrite(A1,LOW);
delay(100);
 lcd.setCursor(0,3);
 lcd.print(" UNAUTHORIZED ENTRY");
 digitalWrite(A2, HIGH);
 delay(150);
digitalWrite(A2, LOW);
 delay(150);
 digitalWrite(A2, HIGH);
 delay(150);
 digitalWrite(A2, LOW);
 delay(150);
 digitalWrite(A2, HIGH);
 delay(150);
 digitalWrite(A2,LOW);
 delay(150);
 digitalWrite(A2, HIGH);
 delay(150);
 digitalWrite(A2, LOW);
 delay(150);
 digitalWrite(A2, HIGH);
 delay(150);
 digitalWrite(A2,LOW);
digitalWrite(A0, HIGH);
delay(3000);
digitalWrite(A0, LOW);
}
delay(200);
}
}
```

You can then run it and try to use the password 1234 to access the system, and use the # to change the password to a new one. It should run successfully, and you will have succeeded in your project. Note that access is granted after the password you type is compared to the password saved in the system, and if the match is okay, access is granted, otherwise, access is denied.

Chapter 7- Weighing Plate

In this chapter, we will create a project to help you weigh things. You should have some experience in soldering. Begin by assembling the following hardware components which are to be used in the project:

- Weighing sensor

- Soldering Iron

- Arduino UNO

- H x 711

Open the Arduino software, and then write the following code in it:

```
#include <Hx711.h>
Hx711 scale(A2, A3);
void setup() {
Serial.begin(9600); }
void loop() {
Serial.print(scale.getGram(), 1);
Serial.println(" g");
delay(200); }
```

Note that we have begun by adding the library for the H X 711. This is the library Hx11.h. You can then wire everything up. The GND on the Hx711 should be connected to the GND on the Arduino board.
The VCC on Hx711 should be connected to the 5v, while the DT on Hx711 should be connected to the A2 and SCK to A3.

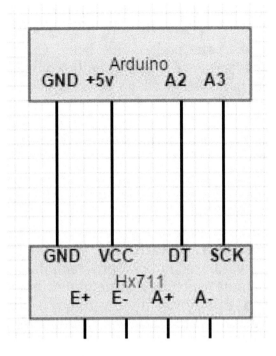

Once you are done with the connections, you can have fun using the app for weighing objects. The Hx711 should be connected to a load cell. Ensure that the connections are done in the correct format, and then have fun using the app.

Conclusion

We have come to the end of this book. One can program Arduino boards so as to come up with complex systems. A good example is a system which controls access to a certain facility, in which you can control the access at the door. If you are familiar with the C programming language, then it will be easy for you to program the Arduino boards. The code is written in the Arduino software, which is open source software. You can download and use this software on your system for free. The codes written in the Arduino software are known as sketches. There are a number of libraries which you need to include in your programs when programming the Arduino board. These libraries are included by use of the "#include" keyword used in the C programming language. You can write programs which can control the Arduino LED's light. Note that you can power the Arduino board from your computer or directly into the power socket, and the effect will be the same in all of these cases. Data can be sent from the computer to the Arduino board and from the Arduino board to the computer. The RX and TX LEDs usually light to show the direction in which the data is flowing.

www.ingramcontent.com/pod-product-compliance
Lightning Source LLC
LaVergne TN
LVHW052315060326
832902LV00021B/3905